SILVER ROSES

Other Books by Rachel Wetzsteon

POETRY

The Other Stars
Home and Away
Sakura Park

LITERARY CRITICISM

Influential Ghosts: A Study of Auden's Sources

Silver Roses

Poems

Rachel Wetzsteon

A KAREN & MICHAEL BRAZILLER BOOK
PERSEA BOOKS / NEW YORK

Persea Books, Inc.
853 Broadway
New York, NY 10003

Library of Congress Cataloging-in-Publication Data

Wetzsteon, Rachel.
 Silver roses : poems / Rachel Wetzsteon.
   p. cm.
 "A Karen & Michael Braziller book."
 ISBN 978-0-89255-364-8 (original trade pbk. : alk. paper)
  I. Title.
 PS3573.E945S55 2010
 811'.54--dc22
                                      2010021060

Designed by Lytton Smith / First Edition
Printed in the United States of America

for WRF

Contents

❧

Foreword by Grace Schulman   xi

I. A New Look

Among the Neutrals   3
Freely from Wyatt   5
A New Look   6
The Wanderer's New Life   8
Time Piece   9
Septimus   10
Algonquin Afterthoughts   11
Pursuits of Happiness   13
Cabaret Ludwig   16
Three Poems after Montale   17
Meditation at Muir Woods   19
The Menaced Objects Series   20
Letter from a Leprosarium   25

II. ENGLISH SUITE

New Journal	29
A Dream Vision	31
Nightingales	32
Rain at Reading	33
A Bedroom in Venice	34
Park-Bench	35
An Actress Prepares	36
A Conjured Rainbow	39
May Poles	40
His Field	42
Compasses	46
The Commission	47
Sotto Voce	50
Mirror Lecture	51
The Bluest Evening	52
Five Finger Exercise	53
Gold Leaves	54
Ferocious Alphabets	55
Ruins	60

III. THE TENNIS COURTS AT STUYVESANT TOWN

MacDowell	63
Halt!	64
Elevator Music	65
Midsummer Night's Swing	66
Exquisite Corpses	67
The Very Rich Hours	68
Interruptus	69
Little Geometry Quiz	70
Mum	71
In a Nutshell	72
Year Zero	73
The Tennis Courts at Stuyvesant Town	75
Paradigm Shift	76
Four First Songs	77
Ex Libris	81
Crepuscule with W.	82
Silver Roses	83

Notes	86
Acknowledgments	87
About the Author	88

Foreword

In these poems, Rachel Wetzsteon writes of love with keen vision and in terrifying depth.

Throughout the book, passionate rhythms surge against received forms. Haiku chains, quatrains, and Sapphics are enlivened with urgent contemporary diction. Skillfully she uses the verse patterns of Donne, Herbert, Pope, and even the likes of Dorothy Parker, whose wit the poet calls on to deride her own sorrow. Like Auden, she mixes elegant speech and low diction, and juxtaposes myths with lively things of her world: Chaplin's *City Lights*, Bleecker Street shops, Rube Goldberg, Panda Chinese take-out, songs at Café Carlyle, a latte on the subway.

Looking outside, searching within, Wetzsteon explores a romance of some three years. In the opening haiku chain, she places herself and her man in a relatively light circle of Dante's hell whose sorry souls had lived without praise or blame, neither pure nor wicked, unlike those lower down who "stood up for something." She recalls:

> Domino-like,
> one "maybe" followed another
> until…all fell down.
>
> ("Among the Neutrals")

Solitude is her sidekick and her demon. At times she mocks it with outrageous laughter and at other times faces its horror. Awake or asleep, dream images pursue her. One passage evokes for me a chapter in *Song of Songs*, in which the lover dreams of running through the streets in search of her beloved. In this poet's dream, she sees her partner

> loom large…until a cruel moon
> spotlights the beast's false joints, and screams
> blast it to shreds, and you come crashing down

into the red-hot waves. Even in sleep
I cannot save you from the carnal deep.

("Three Poems After Montale")

Most striking about this collection, despite the horror, is Wetzsteon's brilliant imagery of light. She sees tendrils vying with "wisps of light," ironically identifying with Sarah Hannah, who, like Wetzsteon, took her own life. She finds

for every tragedy that
pounces at glad gatherings, there are also
radiant beauties

lurking at the edges of cataclysm,
glints of vigor fringing all endings...

("Septimus")

Wetzsteon's title, *Silver Roses*, prepares us for light, and light is everywhere. As in *Sakura Park*, she sets most of the poems in Manhattan; the city streets are, in her eyes, "one vast mirrored surface." The poet reads "a trembling page by rainbow light," and thinks of praise "etching our silver nights and golden days." In a beautiful poem, "Gold Leaves," she writes of an alchemy that can make you step outside

and feel a radiance that was not there
the day before, your sidewalks lined with gold.

"Still persuade us to rejoice," declared W. H. Auden, Wetzsteon's master. And in her poems she admits to "the joy that snuck up when I'd sworn off joy." In her suicide note, she reminded her friends that she had abundant joy in life. She didn't have to remind us. With light pouring forth, even in sorrow, the poems say it all.

—*Grace Schulman*

Silver Roses

I.

A New Look

Among the Neutrals

And I—my head oppressed by horror—said:
"Master, what is that I hear? Who are
those people so defeated by their pain?"
And he to me: "This miserable way
is taken by the sorry souls of those
who lived without disgrace and without praise.
They now commingle with the coward angels,
the company of those who were not rebels
nor faithful to their God, but stood apart.
The heavens, that their beauty not be lessened,
have cast them out, nor will deep Hell receive them—
even the wicked cannot glory in them."

—Dante, *Inferno*, 3.31-42

i.

The ultimate shame:
not even allowed to burn
with other sinners!

ii.

How could we not know
we were drowning in huge tubs
of lukewarm water?

iii.

Tomorrow I choose
has mushroom-clouded into
forever I'm stung.

iv.

Even the poor souls
lower down in the sad wood
stood up for something.

v.

It was a way of
being all things to all men.
But that means nothing.

vi.

Deep misery of
votes not cast, dark memory
of love undeclared.

vii.

Fair velleities
kept us frozen. Do not let
this happen to you.

viii.

Domino-like, one
"maybe" followed another
until…all fell down.

ix.

Through our tears we see
ourselves back on solid ground
making up our minds.

Freely from Wyatt

i.

I have become the forlorn type who buys
almond biscotti for a long night in,
glumly recapturing a sense of sin
through stomach-aches. It hath been otherwise.

ii.

How many times, encountering a line
I like, I long to cry, How like you this?
But my enjoyments arc no longer his
any more than his delights are mine.

iii.

Busily seeking with continual change,
lacking a chamber, naked, meek and sore
of foot, feel free to show up at my door:
I'll find a shawl. I will not think it strange.

A New Look
at Alexander Pope's "Rape of the Lock"

You like it? Gentle mirror, flatter me
With falsehood and forced cheer, but can't you see
A most atrocious crime has been committed
And Justice looks down with her pale brow knitted?
I entered with the boldest of intents,
Full of wild schemes and brave experiments,
For you know me—I love a little change,
I revel in the special and the strange,
But never dreamed I'd exit the salon
With all my happiness and hair quite gone.
I filled Ray's hands with clippings I had brought,
Clear pictures of the kind of thing I sought:
Winona, I insisted, not Sinead.
I feel like Kojak; I wish I was dead.

Tell you what happened? Sorry, I'm aghast;
I'm breathless; it all took place way too fast:
Ray bibbed me, hissed "You'll love it," and was off,
Stopping my mouth each time I tried to cough
A word of protest; then—punch line; don't stir—
Like that intense, high-minded traveler
Realizing he's already crossed an Alp,
I looked into the glass and saw my scalp.
The tears, the screams, the pleas; it was too awful;
Such sheer perversity cannot be lawful,
Satanic Ray declaring "You're so fetching"
While all his minions in the back were retching.

Where have you gone, my late, my golden friends
With all your splendid highlights and split ends?
Why have you hailed, my fair, my trusted Ray,
Such horrors down upon me? You will pay.
(I'll do such things to make you squirm and fret,

Although I don't know what they are just yet.)
   Now I shall bolt my door and be unwell
And learn the hard way how the monkish dwell,
Or else pack up my cares in Samsonite
And wander quickly off into the night.
   No, no, despite this day of dreadful strife
A tiny voice is saying, "Get a life."
The world is over; hairdressers are rats;
But I'll be practical, I'll shop for hats.
I'll roam the stores of Bleecker Street selecting
The broadest-brimmed disguises, and inspecting
The lovely girl with the amazing tresses
Who lets the wind's soft, amorous caresses
Billow her wanton ringlets into space—
Unless they billow back and veil her face.
Unless her long locks, doing what they're bidden
By her own demons, keep the skyline hidden.
Unless—ah me, my thoughts run in a maze;
It's really been the headiest of days—
Her precious curls are snakes in seraphs' clothing,
Gossamer foes who tease her into loathing
The joys and fears of looking at the city;
Unless she's blind as fate, however pretty.
   Saint Joan and Saint Belinda, give me strength;
The Anistons and Paltrows flaunt their length
On giant billboards, and the susurrous
Young Britneys pertly warble, Be like us.
I called their sweet luxuriance my own;
I met my tonsured double with a groan;
But while contentment and clear minds were dozing,
Something was quietly metamorphosing:
Although my new look makes me want to weep, it
Does wonders for my sight. I think I'll keep it.

The Wanderer's New Life

I have wept longer than becomes a man.
My face in the river shows me these
three day's vigil in grim remonstrance—
eyes red, beard beginning, I'm Narcissus'
ugly brother, the one who traveled as far
from water as he could. She's dead to me.
That much I knew when she slipped from my arms
to listen for the cries of the hunter.
And I must die in this muddy river.
One more time I will summon her, that
they may say of me I loved her to the last.
The miller's daughter, let me remember...
a girl who shone, whose eyes slew devils,
who loved me briefly. But suddenly
the maid of the mill is laughable; I see her
pinched-up eyes inspecting the hunter's
clothing, I see them coupling in a haystack far
from her father, and I cannot drown. It is the maid
I loved who's dead; I am free to go. No longer
will I throw my heart into songs that
send her heavenward; I will sing of snow,
of fish, of other things. My faded
miller's slut, I whisper into your ears
this final time the fact that will
reduce you to whorish nothings:
hunters cannot rhyme. The lindens
will be my loves from this day forward,
the river, my goddess; with washed eyes
I will rise from this sluggish bed
where late I moaned and cried. And wander!

Time Piece

My Munch watch screaming
every time I check the time
tells me I'm dreaming

to think I've reckoned
I can shut horror out by
counting each second.

         *   *   *

Yet maybe his roar's
a thunderclap, not a dirge.
Time flies! Time flies! More's

the pressure to know
the sadness of its flight and
make each minute glow!

Septimus

Here's death, she thought, barging into my party,
rusty spikes impaling the grapes and sorbets,
ermine muffs now shining with crisp new menace.
She must assemble,

she must go in, flatter a lord or flirt a
wilting lady back into smiling plumpness;
anything to make the collective daydream
somehow continue.

Still despite her terror she knew one fact and
knew it proudly: for every tragedy that
pounces at glad gatherings, there are also
radiant beauties

lurking at the edges of cataclysm,
glints of vigor fringing all endings—as when,
having laid their dear one to rest, a rainswept
circle of mourners

hangs its numb defeated head low until—whoosh,
crack and flap!—an impudent flock of starlings
plunges up from who can say where, and all eyes
dizzily realize

things that bring shade also are prone to shaking,
falling bodies cannot extinguish new swoops,
and such movements are in the final tally
the things that matter.

Algonquin Afterthoughts

Or else our drunken tumble was
   too true for daylight's pleasure,
too much *in vino veritas*
   troubled the gods of measure
who sent bright draughts of sunshine down
   and sobered up my treasure.

All night rapacity had come
   as naturally as breathing;
we nibbled on each other's necks
   like greedy babies teething.
How soon an empty bottle makes
   one feel a blissful free thing.

"Aspirin, aspirin," he implored;
   I fed him several pills,
and when he wondered where he was
   it gave me frightful chills,
but still I told him of the party's
   unexpected thrills.

Words woke us up, reflection turned
   affection to regret:
"After she left me I tried not
   to do this, but I get
so lonely"…so I showed him out,
   warbling "I'm glad we met."

But now I crave the swift return
   of scotch-transfigured nights,
like Chaplin, horrified by his
   rich friend in *City Lights*
who only recognizes him
   from liquor-gladdened heights,

sticking a tall glass in the man's
   upstanding hand (the clink
or worse awaits poor tramps like us
   if scamps like you won't think)
and meekly scolding, in a voice
   weak with nostalgia, "Drink."

Pursuits of Happiness

i.   Song

—after John Donne and Preston Sturges

Go, and fetch the chilled champagne;
    we have things to celebrate:
you forgave my lust for gain,
    I pardoned you for learning late
that even lady crooks have hearts
      (the memory of it still smarts:
         what snake's
         mistakes
even the brightest young man makes!).

Our raging instant chemistry
    was not enough; you were too young
and bridal-blind, you had to see
    that swindlers also lurk among
women in spun-satin gowns;
      they too have painted sleepy towns
         hot reds,
         their heads—
just like Jean's—dream of rumpled beds.

Someday I will tell you, Hopsy,
    how I wowed the crowd as Eve,
how I turned the world all topsy-
    turvy so you would not leave.
But it's too soon for revelation
    of how I, through a change in station
         and name
         became
positively the same dame.

ii.   The Shower

—after Henry Vaughan and Howard Hawks

Hildy in an apron: well, at first
the idea of it pleased me terribly,
and that man who looks like Ralph Bellamy
     waiting downstairs,
     he really cares
so much about me I'm afraid he'll burst.

But I'm an old newspaperman at heart;
the sound of words colliding with each other
can't be the sort of thing Bruce and his mother
     hear with delight.
     Maybe you're right:
divorce need not be "Till death do you part."

I lay awake at night and thought the clack
of raindrops on the window sounded just
like roaring typewriters; I felt such lust
     to take a tap.
     Come here, you sap,
get off the phone and kiss me hard. I'm back.

iii.   Love (IV)

—after George Herbert and Leo McCarey

When Lucy barged into the mansion claiming
        to be her husband's sister,
she warbled her way through a public shaming
        to make him know he'd missed her.
But we whose loves live far off can't do dances
        demanding second chances.

This is a dance in words, an old flame's joke
        quite soberly intended
to see that pairings that went up in smoke
        are permanently mended
(I hiccup while I sip my glass of pale
        and sparkling ginger ale).

Come with me to Connecticut, dear state
        where everything's the same
yet different, and by midnight we'll deflate
        small cottages of blame
with whirlwinds of grand laughter. Ever your
Lola Warriner.

Cabaret Ludwig

I'll fly off to a fjord in Norway,
post "Oh the pain" above my doorway
if you insist on going your way,
       for this is not a duck.

That is what cowards say, and realists
who run away, shun the appeal its
rare white fur holds, although they feel it's
       a rabbit full of pluck.

Let's multiply, let's twitch our noses,
let's walk among the night's dark roses,
though where the oldest story goes is
       a place where tongues might cluck.

I've had my share of quacks and hisses;
whereof mouth cannot speak, it kisses;
hop to it, man, and realize this is
       a lovely bit of luck.

Three Poems after Montale

i.

Mistletoe, a city of snapshots taped to
plaster, blue bottles and a fire's
fitful sparks the only glimmers
of warmth in your new lodgings.
For you, this season without wreaths,
I would manhandle a city, conjure
a drizzle, then soften it to snow,
paint lampposts deep reds and greens
and so install around your room some
snatches of the festive. But starting
and ending here, these wishes are slipshod:
they never seem to settle on a picture that
touches you at all. Storms, ramshackle
gifts fly freely, but the setting's
the same: you dine upon sausage and frost.

ii.

The violent thrum of error,
the catcalls of the wronged, the small
crimes of a life, and the liquid horror
of crimes to come—all
this gushes and spurts inside
me even in sleep, issuing from a source
I cannot stop anymore. But now, astride
a white-winged, metal horse,
you float above the sea, the dream
takes shape and lets you loom large…until a cruel moon

spotlights the beast's false joints, and screams
blast it to shreds, and you come crashing down
into the red-hot waves. Even in sleep
I cannot save you from the carnal deep.

iii.

Oh, go when you must, but
do not go for long! The place
my thoughts built lingers, but its spirit
is sick; every day new chinks
show on its surface, and mad mouths
surround it, hell-bent on seeing it
crumble. Throw grub at them
as they shriek to keep them happy, distract
them with song, and let this room
continue, this place where a heathen's only
higher hope is realized, where chaos
stays chained, and where your huge,
luminous shadow keeps me agog.

Meditation at Muir Woods

—after Hitchcock's Vertigo

When she walked among
the oldest living things,
fingering the years
with black-gloved sureness,
leaning on dark trees
in spotless white coat,

he didn't know—swooning
in the forest shadows—
whether his throat's lump
meant he stood gazing
at the birth of surging waters
or the grave of impure thought.

The Menaced Objects Series

—after Edward Gorey

i. Used Chewing Gum Set Upon by Unsharpened Pencils

Knowing, as I did,
you'd someday surround me,
did I relish my pinkness,
flaunt my flavor
with sufficient abandon
and gaiety? Did I savor
the moist young mouths and cinema floors
to my last atom
or was I biding time,
squinting at a notional watch and thinking
pop, chomp and blow me senseless,
stick me on an Umbrian hill
or a garret bedpost in Red Hook—
the real fun happens later
when the graphite gang march in to tell my story?
How I loved his tongue's bold questings,
the tug of here,
the lure of legacy leave me breathless.

ii. Domino Intimidated by a Funnel

Flee, flee, dreadful siphoner,
you mess with my content;
my most wide adventures
haven't happened yet.
Without legions more of me
there could be no game;
I was counting on a world

of friends before you came
barging in with bulletins
from the private sphere.
Melancholy Jacques,
bard of all I fear,
take your sole self tapering
to one point, and split.
Solitaire's a sad affair.
There's no point to it.

iii. Formal Glove Being Shone on by a Gibbous Moon

The moon had no answers but it lit up the question:
since you can only pull off a glove so often
before ravishment becomes routine,
since the rapt stares became fond glances,
did ecstasy expire because their love did,
or because its continuation
would mean the ruin of all they wanted to build?
See how slowly the moon caresses every finger.
And see through the window how briskly they manage
their tasks, chopping zucchini, jotting lists.

iv. Cup and Saucer in the Path of a Mechanical Insect

I am, you gush, your "guest,"
and the intimate surroundings
confirm the term—

amid these slouchy sleeves and spread papers
we're all best friends who've never met.
So flow, flow, coffee, over and through us;
make us mirthful, cheerful, raucous, ready for more;
flow from the iPods out to the bean pods and back.
Would I like anything else?
Do you really want to know?
I'd like a public place
where friendship is a slow,
delicate process, something
earned, not instant,
tough, not automatic,
inching by surprise and degrees
toward that amazing confab over cake.
This is my suggestive selling;
this is my hope's bitter knelling
before the cup has done its morning's work.

v. Vase Abandoned on a Permanent Way

Ask me how many rails
lie between me and the shining vistas;
demand of me the precise number of miles
I need to get there quickly, I have the numbers.

But inquire into the glaze,
the fluting, the width of lip
of the vase ever receding—
I scratch my head, I bow it, I cannot say.

vi. Paper Butterfly Apprehensive About Spreading Syrup

Syrup: Spill your secrets, banish secrecy.

Butterfly: That oozing tide would be the death of me,
               beautiful hoardings sluicing down a drain…

Syrup: Paper is what you are and will remain.

vii. Bicycle Wheel Rolling into a Cul-de-Sac

Patience takes practice, and so does practice,
I mused over Panda Chinese takeout
after another meditation class
during which I'd squirmed mightily
but *had* known, two or three times,
those jolts of serene joy
when my slowed mind found itself thinking
fancy this   you are fully content
hearing the distant rustle of trees.

But my snide grimacing
over-cracking of gum, my rage
at ring tones and blaring of whereabouts;
my very short temper
but also my sudden bright cackle;
my crippling familiar obsessions
and monkey's aimless tree-swings: give them up?
If having tics meant, ah, becoming them,
who'd taste the food if the racing tide died down?

viii. Stuffed Toy Being Trifled with by Fire-Tongs

Oh once again this toy I hold, this fine nest we create,
this closeness all the more delicious for arriving late
are prodded, haunted, pierced by doubting voices from the past
who say, Pack up your things and go, this comfort cannot last,
for you are destined now and always for another scene
where you lance boils, sport braces, brood, and wear a size fourteen,
live wholly and quite happily upon an island where
the smallest tender gesture would be more than you could bear.
Oh once again the bad old ghosts have chilled me to the bone;
I wish they'd have the heart to leave my life the hell alone.

ix. Deviled Egg Beneath a Leak Starting in the Ceiling

Beyond this tense table
the hawks and peacocks wander,
the aspens are doing jazz-hands,
the dramas, ignoring you utterly,
feature sky and wind and gorgeous ideas.

Meanwhile the dripping menaces and comforts
with its steady, bounded erosion,
muffles—vain to deny it—the shock
of the greater din outdoors,
slowly aborts the tiny shifts of attention
preceding any radical change.

Letter from a Leprosarium

Dear monologist/friend extraordinaire:

Thank you for the complimentary copy.
We passed it around like smut or chocolate,
sorry only that the lazaretto's
sad lack of bookmarks and gold stars
(not to mention our decaying hands)
hindered our ability to note
our favorite passages. How wrenchingly
you've made a malady a metaphor,
our boils and wails to social awkwardness
perceptively, triumphantly aligned.
Skin clearing up some, wish you were here;
do keep us posted on your future work.
Yours in solidarity,
                           The Lepers.

P.S. How well lies can pass the time.
Now blow the skin-flakes off this stinking page,
squeeze the last dewdrop from your lemon peel,
flop down on your velvet armchair and
take it from us that you have done us wrong,
done us disservice—your props could have been
a kiss, a camera and a stethoscope;
instead you brought a ballpoint and a mirror,
stored both inside that ludicrous black cape,
and when you drove up to the colony
you never left your car. You limned our limbs,
more partial to your punning than our howling;
you nibbled on our necks from far away

and from that distance couldn't know our hair
turns white, not green. We wonder what poor wretch
you'll pick on next; we shiver in the night
when the light dawns that we were never seen.

P.P.S. Come back again someday.

II.

English Suite

New Journal

The inky leaves,
the reams of lamenting
left me angry I was not living, so I left off,
stowed the notebooks with the hotel soaps and mix tapes
in a hard-to-open drawer—

but I could not stay away,
pined for each unwritten-down day

until I caved in, got another,
placed it beside a mug and a candle
on the table by my bedroom window
where now the book is flooding me
with all the ravings it might be:

a pep talk or a picked scab,
a compass or a spigot,
a greenhouse or a trash heap,
a flashlight or a shovel?

An airless room where actors rehearse
for plays that run one night if that,
or a stage on which to get the roles just right?

A chronicle of botched focus
proving nothing but the self's huge shadow—
not moonlight but how I felt in the moonlight?

A box of fantasies or facts,
the salty remarks I wish I'd made
or the leaden ones I did make?

A different sentence to finish each time:
if my mind were a clear glass of water, I'd...?

And was the diary's "dear"
an ideal reader I stretched to impress
or a pale and fatal siren
slowly doling paralyzing poison?

And when I said I "kept" a journal,
did I mean by that prison or salvage?

Spiral-bound quotidiana,
graphic graph-paper confessions
of nights laminated or purged,
lurid or dry recounting
of lists or hopes or errors or dreams,
prized sayings divided by asterisks
or secrets divined by no one,
choose me, impose a method, so that
tonight I write something more
in my brand-new, virginal journal
than *today I bought a journal*;

help me to fill this big blank book of days.

A Dream Vision

Two phantoms came to me one night,

the first a student of opera
and hard knocks; approaching
in a gown spattered by bloodstains,
she bore on a scarlet tray
a gleaming golden pencil, said "Complain."

The second, more flower girl
than demented bride, strewed petals
from bottomless pockets with one hand,
held in the other a purple pillow
with a silver pen upon it, whispered "Praise."

Half-awake in the predawn
I tossed and turned,
raged and burned,
blearily staggered from bed to window
and wondered which fled ghost
would sign her name to the phrases I was forming.

Nightingales

Yes I know what it's from, and so do you,
when after some bird makes a sound outside
you speak of drowsy numbness, and I shoo
the thought away and claim the thing that cried

is day's lark, warming up to travel far.
So carve your chicken, talk to someone else;
our words are getting friendly at the bar,
our legs are making finite parallels...

And is it strange, this cluttered way of talking?
I've always been a sucker for the charms
of influence, benigner form of stalking.
So many clothes you'd think us free from harms!

But layers bring a fine heat, not a numbing.
Now pass the wine and keep the good lines coming.

Rain at Reading

We had gathered under a tent in the park
for some words before lunch and after separate mornings,
and when—twice—the poet said "capital,"
the lightning bolts that followed the noun
had me bolting too; I'd always suspected
God's communist leanings, but now I regretted
how few exchanges we know
between craft and climate:

imagine a rhyme inciting a rainbow,
blood feuds bruising the sky,
hymns of forgiveness bringing a soft
new light to the faces watching the last act,
waltzes and songs and declamations—
this would be capital entertainment!—
locked in a clinch with open air.

But the lightning was as quick as it was loud.
The clouds dispersed,
and then so did the crowd.

A Bedroom in Venice

To snuff a candle out or suffocate
a wife—for him both acts suggested light
extinguished; beasts had horns; and lying conjured
fatal treachery of mouths and beds,
the local meaning and the further one
twin arrows at the borders of a line
he hurried back and forth on, savoring
the bright explosions of these linkages
but also suffering their heat, until
the violent joys and knotted horrors of
his one-man, one-lane highway killed him too.

But we, from sane impulses or faint hearts,
keep deeper senses safely pent, fall down
without invoking apples, rest all night
upon a lover's breast without a thought
of terrifying puns or splendid yokings:

we went to town, and then we went to town.

Park-Bench

(writing firm founded by Dorothy Parker and Robert Benchley)

I sat on one, my hair and spirits wayward,
flaunting my solitude to squirrel and jogger,

> *They formed another, telling a crew*
> *of doubters real and imagined, Damn you:*

safe inside plush Teflon folds
but wondering too about the park's other haunts—

> *our minds meeting will heat this office*
> *and by heat we don't mean splayed limbs*

the playground, the dog run, the pond—and whether
it would be good to seek out company there;

> *or even stolen glances, but rolled sleeves,*
> *brow-sweat and work-lust, delirious neurons,*

such shiftings and such spheres intrigued me,
dream visions of linked arms and passed buckets

> *all other-anguish left at the door,*
> *our goddess not Hymen slayer of brainwaves*

though from the park's edge they seemed so distant,
a whisper about a dream about a rumor...

> *but Hyphen bringer of shared purpose,*
> *a new love song: two typewriters clacking.*

An Actress Prepares

On the film set between takes, she was writing in her journal, *I am coming into my own*

when her leading man sat down beside her and declared his undying love, most confusing words, as he was playing her son,

and so, although she adored him, she said, *More matter with less art,*

wandered the streets for days, seeing lapdogs and chinks in walls everywhere,

thought, *If people were books, who'd cut the pages?*

then immersed herself in her next project, a costume drama in which, in the pivotal duel scene, music swelled as the camera panned past palaces and suburbs and fields to where the two men and she—the winner's prize—stood serenaded by an orchestra in the woods; the soundtrack was theirs too,

causing some to swoon and some to riot,

and sending her home to scribble in her thickening notebook, *Marienbad has nothing on this;*

conceding a need for change

she found dim solace at the gym—Nautilus, Stairmaster, Mobius Strip—

tried poetry, its dizzy truthful feigning,

took up archery and grew smitten with its clean precision, until one overcast afternoon the arrow flew out of sight,

appeared on television that same night, winking at her from an old Olivier film; she recognized its monogrammed shaft, quivered a bit, called her agent,

growled, *Vote me off the island,*

but he rang back seconds later with a stage role she couldn't refuse: the story of her own life.

Rehearsals evoked a vertigo of pride and longing.

She took her curtain calls in character.

People threw roses. The houselights blew a fuse,

though one critic remarked, *I was unpersuaded.*

Leaving the drunken cast to stew at Sardi's, she walked home
in the drizzle, dodging puddles and her own reflection,

though the city streets were one vast mirrored silver surface,

and how stubbornly the small rain down can rain.

A Conjured Rainbow

—in memory of Michael Donaghy

Some radiance had found the little room.
I scrutinized, surrendered to the sight:
my pen (Miss Prism!) made a spectrum bloom,
I read the trembling page by rainbow light.

The moment vanished quickly, slipped into
a past from which, sometimes, it still arrives.
Your tinted poem reminded me of you,
contagious rainbow entering our lives.

May Poles

—in memory of Sarah Hannah

Sarah, the night I learned of you
the Spanish sunset split in two:
since then I've been looking through

blurred windows at a warring sky
where violent crimson tendrils vie
with wisps of light that madly try

to hold onto their fragile piece
of vault despite the fierce increase
of red that lacks the heart to cease.

You knew too well the frail tightrope
between grand plan and slender hope,
scanned buoy, arm and heliotrope

as fish inspect thin strips of sand;
you could not live on this parched land.
But, dear friend fallen, understand

I will not let the velvety
encroachments declare victory;
I will not let the memory

of all your strength and wild delight
be made one micro-beam less bright
by all the bullies of the night.

Instead I'll cast into the air
a picture of your frank wry stare,
a locket of your golden hair,

your poem about the salad days,
and watch these souvenirs amaze
the scarlet henchmen of sad ways

who carved such trenches in your mind
but cannot touch the brilliant, kind
and joyful trace you left behind

or find me nursing the belief
that red's a ruler, not a thief
ruthless in its lust for grief.

Vanished gorse-girl, my first urge is
to despair, but rawness merges
with resolve, and so my dirge is:

let's stare at the setting sun,
hazard an opinion
of who has lost and who has won;

let's regard her lasting spark
and tell the tyrants of the dark
who has left the greater mark.

His Field

i.

Goodbye my follies, my fair-weather friends
he sang, and held the pages high and lit
a match; *for I am struck with the belief*
that I have loved you at an awful cost.
Flames chewed his phrases, wordy curls of ash
grew lacelike in the breeze and spun away.
Plunge like a knife into the thick of things
he said then: but what thickness and what things?
Men wandered past, their bowlers full of holes,
and women crossed the street in ash-smeared boots.
Rush like a beggar after your lost scraps
he thought, afraid, and plucked the poor things back—
a tribute there, a mad rant there—until
his cupped hands held the pages once again
but out of order, in a smoldering
new heap whose damaged words he strained to read.

ii.

He tried to write a story with a storm
so he could feel the flooding all day long,
not only in robust glad dealings with
its watery cousins—weeping, drawing baths

and pouring wine—but during dryer spells,
slow mornings when electric dawns became
grim slabs, and eyes were void as empty wells.
How he had danced and trembled at his plan.

How he had hoped the faces of his friends
would ache and redden, as if struck by hail.
But more and more he shrank away from them,
vicarious and parched, longing for rain,

and looked down with remorse and wonder at
the paper where it always said *Storm still*.

iii.

The day he said farewell to joy, alas,
he sat down at his desk and filled a page:
a pig in clover never learns to fly

And when a bird invited him to fly
he shut his lights and, ghost-pale, wrote "A Lass
Unparalleled" upon a title page.

Finding his door locked, old friends fondly page
and loudly summon him to come and fly
bright kites in meadows, but he cries alas,

alas, the page will perish if I fly.

iv.

Light drizzle was the best the sky could do
all morning, sluggish drops that seemed to say
we'd rather not be coming down, but blue
must get rest too, and wanly does give way
to sour rains that usher in the day
with some half-hearted vague precipitating.
He hurried home and found his inkpot waiting.

The storm he wrote about all night was loud;
it thundered like an ending world, upset
his tablecloth and left his willows cowed.
But ink dried, and he knew authentic wet,
though less exciting, was a better bet.
It always leads to such a messy slaughter,
this war of midnight oil and morning water.

v.

He prowled the picket fence around the pasture,
against the force of new aroma steeled.

Manna too rich for man, he knew, lay waiting
in that green land where more plots were revealed.

There is a most unwholesome kind of sickness
that sees help but refuses to be healed.

("No, no, it is a devil's trick, it wants
to stop my heart for good," he feebly squealed.)

Was it a second Eden where sweet berries
a lavish myrtle's gentle arms did yield?

A bumper crop of purple-gold viburnum
through whose profusion scary insects wheeled?

He took one last whiff of the distant fragrance
and walked away, for it was not his field.

Compasses

My friend told stories I could not believe
of sport among the professoriat,
and toss me clue books if I seem naïve,
dull, spinsterish, inflexible, old hat,

but I'd always assumed that, having taught
of constancy, of compasses that roam
the wide world yet still know true north, men brought
at least a smattering of metal home.

No chance: the only loud sigh-tempests here
were those she could not muffle as she pried
fat gobs of wax from his infected ear;
the only tear-floods anybody cried

were hers, for all that wasted paraffin
lighting up words that never quite sank in.

The Commission

Rube Goldberg met with Cupid in an alley,
said, "Look, I'll help your broken arrow get
to where you want it. First off, let's forget
a mountain's any different from a valley—

we've never heard of obstacles. Next thing,
I'll need a quiet place to work, some room
where I can't hear the roaring traffic's boom.
This attic's perfect. Job well done. Now bring

me earplugs and a crate of beer, then scram."
Cupid obeyed and flew back to his cloud
as Goldberg rolled his sleeves up, and a shroud
of secrecy descended... Leeks, a pram,

dining-room tables and a duck were seen
entering the attic on a pulley
while the paparazzi dutifully
cluttered the corridor where they had been.

Days passed—or were they weeks?—time was a blur
in this electric climate of creation,
just say time passed, when hoots of celebration
coming from the attic caused a stir

among the small dogs on the street below.
Goldberg got Cupid on the phone and said
"I'm going to take the top right off your head:
come quickly to my room so I can show

my latest masterpiece to you." Quaking
with highest hopes and sheer fear, Cupid paced,
put on his darkest sunglasses and raced
into the teeming city, wings aching,

mind afire, and nerves completely raw.
He took the elevator to the ninth floor
where, beaming, Goldberg met him at the door
and let him in. And this is what he saw:

metal and feathers rose up in a narrow
shaft that ended in a triangle
part plywood and part leafy vegetable;
Goldberg had made a statue of an arrow.

Cupid knew Goldberg wasn't serious;
the real contraption waited in the wings!
But when he realized the plain truth of things
he raised his arms and cried out, furious,

"I wanted you to steer a fragile dart
through shark-torn waters and crow-blasted skies
to where my icy-cold beloved lies,
not mock it with this stiff, this ghastly art."

"But frozen sorrow offers such a thrill,"
Goldberg replied, "to those who caused the pain
that motion's loss will be persuasion's gain.
If this doesn't melt her, nothing will."

"Oh Goldberg, Goldberg, would that it were true.
I also used to feel deep in my gut
that works of love could cure indifference, but
I've given that dream up, and so should you.

I wanted rockets surging from the ground.
I wanted pyrotechnics and not planks.
Your artistry's beyond pathetic; thanks
for a great big nothing. See you around."

But Goldberg, not one to be silenced, spent
the next day polishing a marble bow,
and marveled at how Cupid could have so
misunderstood what moving really meant.

Sotto Voce

Well, I could, but I'd
Really rather
Inform you
That your
Expectations

About

Poetry's instant flow are
Odious in the
Extreme:
Majestic moonlight,

Astonishing andantes,
Bad breakups
Obviously call for
Urgent
Treatment, but not yet, only

In
Time.

Mirror Lecture

You've got a brain that travels fast, fine trait
for novel links and sonnets built to last.
How could the roadside poplars know the car
was heating up with stirrings of new love?
But soon a swaying graced an embarkation
with wild encouragement; some sooty clouds
observed one grouchy morning silvered when
the check came in the mail; you read one day
that subtle minds lead lives of allegory
and it was uphill after that—to mounds
of radiant significance, bright peaks
where awkward flailing limbs were suddenly
adorned in velvet sleeves. But down, girl, down:
the journey to this place is full of hazards
much more than occupational: enjoy
the naked fact, the roses at the base
of the enormous mesa. Pause, and look
at all the moment's colors. Breathe, or else
the precious ladder and the swift alembics
will turn on you: your vision in the woods
will go to seed from all the bells and whistles
you've stapled to the tossing trees; too much,
too soon, he'll cry; your nooses are not nice;
I'm wearing socks, not hiking boots, today;
the strawberries I brought for lunch are ripe
because of sun, not us; if little rooms
are everywheres, the air gets awfully musty—
at which dire words you cower and look frightened,
twirling your eternal golden braids.

The Bluest Evening

"I'm writing titles with two tentacles."
"Last time I checked, songs were not octopi."
"Scoff if you like, I'm speaking not of squid
but stretchability; I'm on the prowl
for lyrics looking back and looking forward
so any evening when you sing the tunes
all time is yours, known, captured: In the Still
of the Night and Day; The Way You Look Tonight
Won't Be Just Any Night; Kind of Blue Moon.
The Café Carlyle's windows would look out
on scenes from childhood, and on heads of grey!"

Five Finger Exercise

When things get hot and heavy this weekend or one August
    twenty years from now and I start tapping hexameters
up and down the shoulder-blades of my beloved (insert
    auspicious, trustworthy-sounding, stolid but fun name here
for I can conjure none), I hope I do it right,
    never losing sight of the skin whose golden toughness
allows the counting, never moving my fingers so briskly
    that I can't hear his breathing, and never forgetting, even
in the lonely heights of sublimest inspiration—
    What is your substance?... *O rose...and grey and full of sleep*—
to flip the warm flesh over and whisper, *It had to be you.*

Gold Leaves

Someone ought to write about (I thought
and therefore do) stage three of alchemy:
not inauspicious metal turned into
a gilded page, but that same page turned back
to basics when you step outside for air
and feel a radiance that was not there
the day before, your sidewalks lined with gold.

Ferocious Alphabets

i   .

Are you
Brave enough to
Concede that
Diligence isn't
Enough? What's the trip
For if you
Glide so
Hastily forward that
Icicles' spangles,
Jelly beans'
Kelly greens
Leave you cold?
Missing out on
Nice
Or
Profound
Qualities—you Mr.
Ramsays aside,
Striving
To finish what you
Urgently began—is
Very
Worrisome (though
X-tra! X-tra! I'm done!
You cry
Zealously).

ii.

"A," I
Blurted when
Certain
Doubting
Ethereal
Forms,
Grinning
Hugely,
Inquired
Just what
Kind of
Letter described
My type.
Now
Observe, one
Proffered
Quietly,
Rachel
Succumbing
To
Underachievement:
Vain labor
With Whiteout and
X-Acto knife erased,
You could really
Zoom in on things.

iii.

All right:
Begin again, mimicking
Clouds'
Drift,
Egrets' slow
Foraging,
Gurus'
Herculean calm.
Isn't it better?
Jolly good;
Kudos to this
Loitering, I
Mutter; but my heart's
Not in it:
Only by
Pressure,
Querulous,
Raging and
Self-imposed, can I
Trample
Ugly
Verities, though deaf to
Warbles of
Xylophones,
Yodels,
Zithers.

iv.

A
Bard once
Cozily
Declared that
Earth's the right place
For love—
Good for
Him. But
I'd grown
Jaded,
Killed my
Last
Molecule of
Naturally
Occurring
Passion.
Quackery,
Really, I
See
These days—
Uranus isn't
Very
Warm, and
X-rated hopes,
Yellow hairs still thrill me,
Zut and alas…

v.

And so,
By hook or by
Crook I
Developed
Eyes
For
Gazing, my
Hearing
Improved, the
Jambalaya and
Kale I
Lingeringly
Munched in
New Orleans
Offered new
Pleasures.
Quarries of
Realer
Satisfaction
Tumbled their
Unforeseen
Valuables
When I said,
"X, Y, Z,
You've been
Zapped."

Ruins

I sat on the subway sipping latte,
reading a short history of ruins.

Then, boarding the bus at Ninety-Sixth Street,
grabbed by mistake—such screwball
anti-élan!—a blind man's cane
instead of the post beside his slouching form.

Then home to my journal and ordering in.

There are times when one feels oneself
the star of a movie about one's life,
all nuance and dimension replaced
by scare-quote features, floodlit in plain day.

There are times when one feels a frightful cliché.

And yet the coffee tasted good,
the book set me brooding helplessly,
hopefully, on the folly of recent woes.

To every cliché, a germ of truth.
To do otherwise, a terrible falsehood.
And so, to the unthumbed cookbooks,
to the lavender lipstick bought
in a you-must-change-your-life frenzy,

a gentle *not yet*: this caffeine high,
this madcap tribute to Hepburn's ghost,
this zeal for aqueducts and abbeys
compose a life, though someday they may rest
in cobwebbed attics, dear ruins of former selves.

III.

THE TENNIS COURTS AT STUYVESANT TOWN

MacDowell

For once I fought back,
answering, *Oh yes, someday*
when a restless muse asserted
This golden age needs treatment on the page.
It was the strangest lesson—
all that ink to make me think
shadows were real, this silence
when one true heart so manifestly was.
Time passed. Themes amassed;
I scoffed at amber, basked in oxygen.
Now in this little cabin
where no sightings slake my cravings
and my pen gets back its need to conjure,
on the ingots I have stored, oh pine, opine.

Halt!

And here am I with my idiot humming
who for so long, sad flaneuse, careened
through those dark caves of love and work,
that twilit part with its blossoms

that came and went like fugitive suitors.
I knew the part by heart, but now
my flashlight finds safe passage,
the sprigs you bring keep blooming

and who's this in the mirror with
her willow cabin swept out to sea?
I must face my fate like Estragon, asking,
What do we do now, now that we are happy?

Elevator Music

A slam without a goodbye,
and pangs of the world ending
by the sixth-floor elevator
until you run out, arms extended,
and moist eyes meet moist eyes
as the tough old globe spins on.

Anger's a thing of darkness, but
forgiveness is Shakespearean: it calls for
gardens and dances, lanterns strung from trees
I am no dancer, so instead I'll tell you

that rage, like everything else of late,
has suffered a sea change: no longer
a bleak Bermuda Triangle
in which my flailing ardor drowned,
it's a bit of trash, a bottle cap
bobbing on gentle waters—
much like the way this awful plaid carpet
absorbs a tear that will have dried
next time the elevator brings me here.

Midsummer Night's Swing

One must live in the present tense,
observed Bette Davis, but I have
always lived in the present
tensely. Tell me
about it: two absent-minded sisters,
backward-peering and future-ogling,
took turns obscuring my vision,
and if managed a brief repose
I did it awkwardly:
my senses somehow took their pleasures
smoke and mirrorishly.

But you don't have that problem, so
train your gaze with ferocious glee,
sway your body gently
to the Dirty Dozen Brass Band
heating up Lincoln Center Plaza
and, hearing the tuba's boom,
I'll try to do the same,
for I scribbled vainly all afternoon
and later will be lovely,
but so are these current presents
that make this, for now, the only concert—
trumpet, sky, fountain, dancing eyes.

Exquisite Corpses

A long day sunk in old ways:
my corpus needs a core, but when
I draw the blinds and strip I find
not pearls, but panic, a voice
telling me for the thousandth time
the sole self drowns in freedom, cries all night.

With what giddy gratitude then
do I hop the A train, descend
to a web of pleasure and duty
where I cannot work alone,
whether watching a double bill or
making exquisite corpses with your son:

he does the head, folds it, passes it,
I trace a torso, he sketches thighs,
I add the feet—and oh my darling
we cannot enter each other's minds
but our motives hum and work together,
form a whole body when the drawing's done.

The Very Rich Hours

Your keychain and old watch,
dangling from a belt hoop, suggest
Proust on love: space and time made
directly visible to the heart.

But get a better timepiece,
sort the openers from the metal
that unlocks nothing, and I won't complain
of metaphors untimely ripped;

for thievish seconds need counting
and real doors need moving through,
despite the irresistible storehouse
of stories that attend on you.

Interruptus

There was a lull, a break from bliss
when I turned to face the window
looking for all the world, you said,
"like I was composing a new verse."

Even on our pleasure barge
there are lapses in understanding,
for this groping for words (I thought but did not say)
is not a gasp for air but a further plunging;

I stroke you with both tangible hands
and feet unstressed or thudding...
but "sorry, love" did seem in order
before the revels resumed. Or continued.

Little Geometry Quiz

If faced squarely,

is this triangle's third side
on which chatter and lurk your old loves—
the potheads and Grace Kelley dead ringers,
the tall rich sylphs, doctor-players,
mope rockers and philosopher queens—

something I'd see crushed?
If they vanished, would the line become
a newly firm base we viewed
as we flew like a flexible hinge
or carefree bird to wide skies?

Or would we collapse on the instant
like a tent in trouble,
the harem in hindsight the very haven
I'd thought I sought, the smiles that plagued me
the pain that kept the passion going?

I who was once good at math
a hop and a jump from your house
come up short, madly circle the question
but despair of an answer, hoping at least

the fact that a triangle
is percussive but also tuneful
will make the music of the brooding sweeter.

Mum

Call it saving face—
all that time I spent
pumping oxytocin
when I should have sprayed mace

I can't share with you,
unless nebulous tales
of gashed receding sails
qualify as true.

No one wants to hear
Not until now have I
fallen and been caught by
such wide arms. But we're

(call it safe to bet)
not in any hurry;
every last sob story
will sail from these lips yet.

In a Nutshell

Reliving, I guess, old harms from a safe perch
I concocted such carnage those first months,

crunching bones and mutilations
and carving of guts—do they give an award,

a REMmy, to the scariest one?—alternating
with brutal if less messy betrayals until

purged, I suppose, or simply weary
of horror shows with no cause, no cause

(my cold sweats catapulted me
to your warm arms, reliably)

I got back rest and whimsy one night
in a lovely vision of infinite space:

from a curb we surveyed the city,
giddy but serene, on roller skates.

Year Zero

Boil down the years until they become
a sordid bolus, a rotten bundle,
and throw the grim thing out with tomorrow's trash.

Collapse the bars where you drank too much
(mistaking a lunge for a loving touch),
the masked balls you supposed were come-as-you-are,
until they form one lurid snapshot:
a lot of people standing in a kitchen.
Tear it up by the river one spring dawn.

Raze the chamber where the Brahms piano music,
yearning and yearning outside the window,
nearly drove you mad that summer,
the railroad flat where the roommates took turns
questioning life's joy and purpose;
stand beside the space you've cleared,
say, "On this rock I build a lasting structure."

Pile high the letters sent and received,
then strike a match and cackle wildly
as pleas and feints and imprecations
melt into what you'd have known they were
if you'd only kept your head on: laughable ash.

But the very sad Intermezzo,
the ill-judged apple martini,
the plunges fueled by false trust
and misted mirrors are destroy-proof;
they hover at the edges of freshness
as relieved comparisons or, sometimes, bad dreams—

sign perhaps that a truly blank slate's
for amnesiacs and empty classrooms,
a purge that cannot prove how far you've come.

The Tennis Courts at Stuyvesant Town

Before, there was a longing—pock—
conjured by lack or hope,
and the ball sailed out to the day's landscape,
came back as sharpened senses, bluer views.

But here in Stuyvesant Town
the tennis courts are real,
real too (my memoir: from crossed stars
to crossed fingers?) this sturdy hand I grip.

And I, for far too long
for comfort having found warped comfort
in the sports coach-cinematographer
ruling my brain, I roam with you

like an alien in a new world,
con the part clumsily;
if I must succumb to metaphor
let me see the net and asphalt

as an enduring endeavor
of sweat, botched serves and ever-better volleys,
and always the ball going back and forth in sunlight.
At forty I am learning to play tennis.

Paradigm Shift

It will not last, this blip of warmth—
misanthropy my default mode, my armor—
but as I head east to love and banter,
to rum and orange juice and a triple feature,
Lizzy leaves the room, and another Bennet sister
rushes in and regards
the surging hearts in stilettos,
the pie-eyed misfits on stoops,
the silent couple nursing grudges,
the desperati outside the bar
waiting for something wonderful to happen,
and I find myself agreeing
with Jane: if only everyone could be
so happy.

Four First Songs

i.

Was it better
when, our first embrace
heralding the dawn of
every bright thing, we believed
the other's perfect love
copied a dream's grace
        to the letter?

Or did our sighs
and smiles grow more true
once we'd journeyed, learned, fought,
discovered ourselves deceived
by ideals cheaply bought,
and then gazed into
        real flaws, real eyes?

ii.

I was born in the autumn
after the Summer of Love,
and since then I've fallen hard for fall;

more than probably was
altogether healthy,
told October, *take your sweet time dying.*

After August's onslaught,
June's loud fleshy raptures,
here were my moods mapped and matched and sanctioned—

hue and rue began a
melancholy tango
up and down the red- and gold-lined drive

while I flourished, chanting
masochistic ditties:
yes, remind me, do, that all things wither.

But when someone came and
held me close and made me
see the glibly gloomy girl I was,

all my morbid mirrors
trembled, shifted, shattered;
I still greet the elegiac elms

with excited cheeks and
strange dramatic cooings,
but what I adore about their leaves

in their final stages
has evolved, has softened:
now you know, they whisper, *what it is*

not to want this finite
finery to vanish;
now I love the gold but not the going.

iii.

Bunched handkerchiefs lie scattered on the floor;
ghosts linger, though they left and slammed the door.
   Save your sorrow; no one likes a raver.

You dither while I storm and call you lazy;
my penchant for right angles drives you crazy.
   Save your sorrow; do flawed selves a favor.

The bower has become a well-lit room;
I balk at this, succumbing to dumb gloom.
   Save your sorrow; each phase has a flavor.

My laciest aubade is marred by sirens;
we do each other foolish mental violence.
   Save your sorrow; this is absurd behavior.

There may be trials, and horrible diseases;
can you lie back and realize how good ease is?
   Save your sorrow; these are the days to savor.

iv.

The world had fled, with all its silly cares
and questionable aches, and in one swoon
we rose above its stupefying airs
like flying lovesick pigs up to the moon.
    In that blue light where two lives equaled all,
    our souls looked down upon a spinning ball.

The world returned, and this was a surprise
I raged against like someone on a rack,
telling the sun, tears clouding my stunned eyes,
give us our splendid isolation back.
    I craved third rails, a shot of something strong
    when I found out it doesn't last for long.

The world came back and stayed, pain never ended,
but when the aches and cares begged for a hand,
grew softer in the light we'd made and tended,
I finally began to understand
    love's widening third stage, and of the three
    this was the most outstanding ecstasy.

Ex Libris

Awkwardly I'm learning,
like heliotropes turning
away from rancid meadows
to where the sun is burning...

Ballpoint in hand
I mourned corpses by moonlight,
cooed at sightless embryos
safe in their petri dishes

until these sad rites came to feel
as natural as breathing.

Perhaps they were natural.

But so is breathing
and so is praise,
etching our silver nights and golden days.

Crepuscule with W.

Dusk and a walk and (cue trombones) a weird new absence of
angst, which void I promptly filled with a tangle of worried
beads, most especially that a friend had said the other day, almost
by way of congratulation, *Your emotional life is over.* Already
I could see myself heading out into one of the rainstorms I'd
loved all my life—oh trouble and kiss and cleanse me—beneath
cotton-lined slicker and duck umbrella. Or else, hypothetical
stupor, we could go see the Golden Doors at the Met, but why
bother when these five rooms are gilt, are entrance enough?
And further, darker: when I hauled my bags from Frostbite Falls
to Harmony Hall, did the decline of menace mean the advent
of bland gladness? Did I leave behind (the biggest bead, the
plaintive saxophone solo) a woeful but working mind, and would
the dusks be different from this night forward? *Colpo di fulmine,*
shiver of spine, gentle late light, companion mine, play our cards
right and the answer will be a frail but definite probably: they
will be orange and red and purple still, with (face it?) less extreme
but subtler, deeper hues. Here's comfort for two in twilight,
here's hoping here's heartening news for clasped hands venturing
into the world, the world…

Silver Roses

The strings, as if they knew
the lovers are about to meet, begin
to soar, and when he marches in the door
they soar some more—half ecstasy, half pain,
the musical equivalent of rain—
while children who have grown up with one stare
steal further looks across a crowded room,
as goners tend to do.

My father loved it too,
warned me at dinner that he'd be a wreck
long before the final trio came
(*Ja, ja*, she sighed, and gave him up forever);
he found his Sophie better late than never
and took the fifth about his silent tears
but like him I'm a softie, with a massive
gift for feeling blue.

I went with others, threw
bouquets and caution to the whirling wind,
believing that the rhapsody on stage
would waft its wonders up to our cheap seats;
but mirrors can be beautiful fierce cheats,
delusions of an oversmitten mind;
I relished trouser roles until I had
no petals left to strew.

Up, down the avenue
I wandered like a ghost, I wondered why
a miracle is always a mirage,
then plodded home and set back all the clocks,

spent hard-won funds installing strong new locks,
telling myself if violence like this
could never sound like violins, I would
to art, not life, be true.

And I am trying to
fathom the way I got from there to here,
the joy that snuck up when I'd sworn off joy:
we've made a sterling start, we've got a plan
to watch it on your satin couch downtown
and I'll be there upon the stroke of eight,
bearing in my trembling ungloved hand
a silver rose for you.

Notes

"Letter from a Leprosarium" is a response to my poem "A Leper in the City" (*The Other Stars*, Penguin 1994).

"May Poles": for the phrase "gorse-girl" I am indebted to the poet Eva Salzman and Sarah Hannah's own poem "You Furze, Me Gorse."

Acknowledgments

Thanks to the editors of the following journals, where some of the poems in this collection first appeared:

Barrow Street: Meditation at Muir Woods; *Big City Lit*: May Poles; *Cimarron Review*: Ferocious Alphabets (i and v); *Columbia Magazine*: The Commission; Ruins; Time Piece; *Cortland Review*: Five-Finger Exercise; Gold Leaves; *Literary Imagination*: Among the Neutrals; Pursuits of Happiness; *The New Republic*: The Wanderer's New Life; *The New York Sun*: The Bluest Evening; Nightingales; *PEN America*: A New Look; *Poetry*: Algonquin Afterthoughts; Cabaret Ludwig; Four First Songs (iv); Rain at Reading; Silver Roses; *Raritan*: Three Poems after Montale; *The Threepenny Review*: A Bedroom in Venice; *The Yale Review*: Freely from Wyatt.

Gratitude also goes to the MacDowell Colony and William Paterson University for their generosity to the author. Thanks too to the Center for Book Arts, which printed "Nightingales" as a limited-edition broadside in 2006; this poem was also reprinted in the 2009 Alhambra Poetry Calendar.

About the Author

Rachel Wetzsteon (1967–2009) is the author of three previous poetry collections, including *Home & Away*, *The Other Stars*, and *Sakura Park*, as well as a critical study of W. H. Auden. Her poems regularly appeared in leading magazines and journals, among them *The Nation*, *The New Yorker*, *The Paris Review*, *Poetry*, and *The Yale Review*. She received numerous awards, grants, and fellowships, including the Witter Byner Prize from the American Academy of Arts and Letters; taught at William Patterson University and the Unterberg Poetry Center at the 92nd Street Y; and was poetry editor at *The New Republic*. She lived in the Morningside Heights neighborhood of New York City.